NO BOSSES ALLOWED

Lead to Serve and Transform

Yvette C. Owens

Legal Disclaimer

Connect with MPowered Voice Publishing
www.MPoweredvoicepublishing.ca

Introduction

Welcome to the insights that will equip you as an exceptional leader and be recognized as an influential individual who shapes the culture of successful teams and organizations. Leaders enter every leadership opportunity engaging diverse minds, personalities, and perspectives to the desired outcomes every time.

I am known as the "Business Ambassador." I help leaders build strong, healthy cultures inclusive of developing the individual and organization simultaneously through leadership development. Healthy cultures are never realized through bossy leaders. However, leaders committed to serving and transforming the organization and every individual engaged in the journey experiences longevity and greater profitability on all levels.

In "No Bosses Allowed || Lead to Serve and Transform," you will learn what is required for today's leaders to be successful in a culture challenged by elevated social-economic injustices, a pandemic, and financial challenges.

Table of Contents

Contents

Individuals Matter

Position #1:

Bosses use, overlook and discredit individuals. They are focused on how to bring success to the organization, so they selfishly benefit. Bosses primarily seek to rule and control individuals and situations.

Leaders value the team members and expect the talent to enable the desired outcome — the individual and all that is important to those individuals matters to the leader. Your team will do their best when they know you recognize and appreciate them individually for who they are total.

I have the privilege of getting to know some fascinating people with complex stories. We share our experiences, thoughts and collaborate on a design. We appreciate our unique qualities. No one is denied because the sum of our experience is the currency supporting our future joint ventures. It is safe to share lessons and practices learned due to the environments in which we grew up. It all counts — our education, faith practices, recreation, vacations, and prior work assignments. Does your culture give each person the freedom to express their authenticity? Is everyone encouraged to become better people, create better products and services, and build more substantial businesses?"

The freedom of experience starts with respect for one another and openness to have biases challenged or, better yet, dispelled. Oxford Languages dictionary defines 'bias' as "a prejudice in favor of or against one thing, person, or group compared with another, usually in a way considered to be unfair." Tucking away or denying biases is wasteful and negligent. Once you acknowledge that you have biases, you learn what they are when situations trigger your biases to activate. Every human desire is to be understood and accepted. Open the door to gain respect for the members of your team. Everyone exists for a purpose. Will you confirm and support your biases by continuing in the same behavior or overcoming your biases by exploring more to silence your biases?

Investigate the root cause of your biases, the application, and its implication to your current relationships. Choosing a go-forward response is not always easy. You may encounter pain, hurt, and shamefulness as you become more aware of your bias. Beating yourself up for having a tendency is not the objective. Recognizing the bias exists and committing to facing it head-on to manage it is an appropriate response.

Bosses do not listen when people try to talk with them about anything outside of what interests the boss. Bosses bark orders at people. Everything is about the boss. The boss's concerns, questions, and desires are the only things that matter. Their attitude is that we hired you to do a job, and we pay you. It would be best if you did not look for or expect anything else. The boss asks, "Why is anything other than a job and pay necessary to create a good human experience?" The boss believes that anything other than a paycheck for completed assignments just gets in the way of doing business. The truth is that people only give a small percentage of themselves to tasks where they are unappreciated. Leaders, you want your entire team to think of possible growth and enjoying fulfillment in the workplace. Working with you and the group should never be only a means to pay the bills and provides for their families.

Most individuals are not aware of their purpose and gift to the world. Living a life of survival is all many people expect; to be educated, work, and hopefully, retire with some years left to enjoy before death. Leaders help individuals see that there is so much more to why they are here, breathing and producing. Leaders have an expressed expectation that every team member is identifying and using their exceptional qualities for the benefit of the organization and beyond.

Without proper coaching, it is not easy to discover your purpose. Proper guidance does not tell you who to be, what to do, or where to study. Leaders coach by providing the structure for individuals to explore and understand their strengths and purpose. You enable the person to make the best decisions for themselves, despite what everyone else thinks. Leaders desire to work with people who own and are pursuing their purpose. Individuals living through their purpose choose work, training, and networks to empower them every moment.

Meet each person where they are with the intent of showing them their more significant potential and opportunities. Individuals must decide how far they will go. Organizations often choose for their employees how far they can grow by limiting access to opportunities. The limited access often stems from assumptions made through biases around age, gender, race, faith, nationality, outside interests of their employees, family dynamics, and many more attributes of their team members. Not taking the time to have meaningful conversations with your team members regularly makes it highly challenging to make decisions or recommendations about someone's future.

Every individual is essential, people of color, white, female, male, those born in your country or elsewhere, those practicing a different faith, those physically challenged or struggling with confidence. Transformation comes as you commit to allowing everyone to be their best and grow into their better as they add to the group's success.

Chapter Summary:

This chapter explores the stark contrast between bosses and leaders in terms of their attitudes and behaviors towards individuals. Bosses are depicted as self-serving, focused on control and disregarding the unique qualities of team members. On the other hand, leaders are portrayed as valuing their team members, recognizing, and appreciating them individually. They create an environment that encourages personal growth and authenticity, where biases are challenged and respect is fostered. The chapter emphasizes the importance of understanding and overcoming biases, acknowledging everyone's purpose, and providing coaching and opportunities for individuals to discover and fulfill their potential.

Recommended Action Plan:

1. Recognize biases: Take time to reflect on personal biases and acknowledge their existence. Understand how biases can affect relationships and decision-making processes.

2. Investigate root causes: Dig deeper into the root causes of biases and their implications in current relationships. Explore personal experiences, upbringing, education, and cultural influences that may have contributed to biases.

3. Face biases head-on: Commit to managing biases by actively working to overcome them. Be prepared for potential discomfort, as becoming more aware of biases can be challenging. Remember that the goal is to manage biases, not to beat oneself up for having them.

4. Foster respect and openness: Create an environment of respect where team members feel safe to express their

authenticity. Encourage open dialogue and challenge biases through meaningful conversations.

5. Coach individuals: Provide guidance and structure for individuals to explore their strengths and purpose. Empower them to make decisions that align with their own aspirations, regardless of external expectations.

6. Create equal opportunities: Avoid limiting access to opportunities based on assumptions or biases. Regularly engage in meaningful conversations with team members to make informed decisions about their future growth and development.

7. Embrace diversity: Recognize the value of every individual, regardless of their background, race, gender, faith, nationality, or other attributes. Commit to creating an inclusive environment where everyone can contribute to the success of the group.

8. Encourage personal growth: Help individuals discover their purpose and unique gifts. Support them in choosing work, training, and networks that empower them to reach their full potential.

By implementing these actions, leaders can foster a culture that values and appreciates individuals, encourages personal growth, and ultimately leads to the success of the organization and the well-being of its team members.

Create your personal 90-Day Action Plan:

1)

2)

3)

4)

5)

Care for Communities

Position #2:

> *Bosses are insensitive to the condition of the communities represented by their team. They do not care about what happens in the lives of those they are leading. Nothing matters other than what you can do to help me succeed.*

> *Leaders understand that the whole person comes to work every day. They are aware of how well the organization serves those communities, if at all, and what significant events are taking place in those communities.*

In 2020, it became apparent that leaders at all levels of organizations had no clue how it was to be Black, Hispanic, or Asian in America. Leaders were unaware of individuals from different races, nationalities, religions, and gender experience daily in the workplace. Microaggression is real and prevalent. Insensitive comments, decisions, and behaviors add to the struggles of those underserved in our country. Bosses say, "Business is business, and what happens outside this organization should not impact your performance." Leaders step up to learn more and remain in touch with the plight of the communities represented on their teams. Leaders look for a way to help make life easier in those communities. At the very least, leaders insist the entire team increases their capacity to discuss the issues faced in various troubled communities openly.

Members view their leaders through the lens of questions such as those listed below.

- How can you care about me and not even be aware of or slightly interested in the things that matter to me most?
- Can there be a real connection between us when you are not aware of my community?

Some are trying to work through the issues they face, while others are looking for an escape. Your team wonders how to interact with teammates from communities struggling. More of them are on edge as to what they can say and what they cannot say. Walking on eggshells is never fun. Life is more intense as scenarios like those listed below become public and the cry for justice amplifies. Leaders openly acknowledge the circumstances and create a space for all perspectives to be discussed and respected. Consider the impact of the following situations on your team's performance and how you will make that safe space for reflection and healing.

- Poor water quality in Flint, Michigan
- Political unrest in Israel.
- George Floyd's death in Minnesota
- Countless crimes against Black, Asians, Indians, and others across the USA
- School shootings and other attacks on our children in schools and universities
- Irregular weather patterns such as:
    - Ice Storms in Texas
    - Fire Storms on the West Coast
    - Hurricanes in the Dominican Republic
    - Earthquakes in Haiti
- Children left at the USA Border without their parents
- Destruction of the farming industry in the USA
- Devastation due to the pandemic.
- Increased lack of food, housing, and jobs
- Political division in the USA
- Muslims, Jews, and Christians are under attack

Real-life happens to the people on your team. Extending conversation beyond the work and the work environment can appear tricky. You may be great at leading your team assignments, goals, and objectives. There is so much more that directly and indirectly dictates your decisions and behaviors. What you learn about another person is seen through your influencers' filter. Caring about each other's communities is critical in creating a culture for your team to succeed as a high-performing team. Why? Your thoughts, speech, and behaviors are all influenced by what you experience. Your approach to work shifts as the intensity of your life shifts. Life is tense for many now. People monitor the amount of time they watch the news or social media to avoid bitterness and hostility. It is a real struggle. While bosses do not care, leaders must be sensitive and aware of the impact on each member of their team.

Show interest in your staff outside of the organization. Knowing whom they do life with and how they view those relationships provides information on significant events that will take place. We all experience life events differently, but the circumstances are similar and great places to bond and create a sense of belonging. Focus on the similarities you have while celebrating the differences. You will enhance your perspective and reduce biases. Feeling connected goes far beyond "fitting" in. Honored as a vital member of the team is the most flattering level of belonging.

Expanding your learning of the communities that your teams come from does not mean you agree. You will have a better understanding as opposed to assuming from afar. It is not about a Christian trying to convert a Muslim or a feminist trying to influence a dominant male. When we appreciate each other's differences and learn how to communicate effectively through our differences, our work's outcome will be far superior. Respect and care about your team members just as much as you care about the team's performance.

Chapter Summary:

This chapter highlights the stark difference between bosses and leaders when it comes to their awareness and sensitivity toward the communities represented by their teams. Bosses are depicted as indifferent and unconcerned about the lives and struggles of their team members outside of work. In contrast, leaders recognize the importance of understanding and being involved in the communities their team members come from. The chapter emphasizes the need for leaders to be aware of and address issues faced by underserved communities, create a safe space for open discussions, and show genuine care and interest in the personal lives of team members.

Recommended Action Plan:

1. Increase awareness: Educate yourself about the experiences and challenges faced by different races, nationalities, religions, genders, and communities. Stay informed about current events and issues affecting these communities.

2. Foster open discussions: Create a safe and inclusive environment where team members feel comfortable discussing their experiences and concerns related to their communities. Encourage open dialogue, active listening, and respect for diverse perspectives.

3. Acknowledge real-life events: Recognize that team members are impacted by significant events happening in their communities. Be aware of local, national, and global issues that may affect their well-being and performance. Show empathy and support.

4. Extend care beyond work: Show genuine interest in the personal lives of your team members. Get to know their families, friends, and communities. Understand the significant events and celebrations in their lives. This builds connections and a sense of belonging.

5. Embrace differences: Appreciate and celebrate the diversity within your team. Focus on similarities while respecting and valuing differences. Foster an inclusive environment where team members feel valued for their unique contributions and perspectives.

6. Challenge assumptions: Avoid making assumptions about team members based on their backgrounds or communities. Seek to understand their experiences through meaningful conversations and learning. Avoid imposing your beliefs or trying to change others but rather focus on effective communication and understanding.

7. Prioritize respect and care: Demonstrate respect, care, and empathy towards your team members. Show that you value them as individuals and genuinely care about their well-being. This enhances team morale and creates a positive work environment.

8. Continual learning: Commit to ongoing learning and self-reflection. Continually seek to expand your knowledge about different communities and cultures. Challenge your own biases and assumptions to improve your leadership effectiveness.

By implementing these actions, leaders can foster a culture of understanding, inclusivity, and care within their teams. This will not only enhance team performance but also create a sense of belonging and well-being among team members.

Create your personal 90-Day Action Plan:

1)

2)

3)

4)

5)

Aspire to Inspire!

Position #3:

> *Bosses are assignment and task-focused. They care about your learning more only to enhance your job performance. They are not interested in your skills or knowledge being transferable.*
>
> *Leaders encourage individuals to become intimate with their most vital skills, talent, and competencies to align them with their life's purpose and become the best version of themselves.*

Leaders care about their team's success personally and professionally, and that care is felt and heard in every interaction. Conversations with you should not start and end with your impressions of where and how an individual should develop. Seek first to understand what the individual desires to achieve—the individual and the organization benefit when you encourage transparency of personal goals. Your team will excel when their passion and purpose are activated. Ask the members of your team, "Why did you choose to join this organization, and what would you like to get from this community?" "How does your role in this organization add to your personal goals for strategic growth?" Expect an answer — partner with and coach anyone not ready to answer to help them respond to the questions.

Know the goals of the individuals on your teams and inspire them to achieve their goals as they complete their assignments. Create opportunities for your team members to work in projects or groups to utilize and enhance their skills. Holding onto anything too tight strangles the life out of it. A person's passion will diminish when you keep people suppressed in positions.

Allowing members of your organization to spread their wings and soar does not equate to exiting the organization. In many cases, loyalty and endearment increase as individuals can explore right where they are.

Will some of your team still leave the organization after giving them the freedom and support to shape and build their skills? Yes. It is excellent when individuals go under favorable circumstances. You gain an external ally adding to your professional community. People rarely forget those who helped them. Be a helping hand to many.

As a leader, how do you inspire others to benefit the individual and the organization? Below is a list of ways to inspire others.

1. **Model the inspiration** you aspire to promote. People are always watching you. Be your best self, let your reputation, character, and behavior speak well of you, and inspire others to do the same.

2. **Be transparent** in sharing your success, failures, and how you overcome disappointments while remaining consistent in your character and behavior. Your story is powerful and allows others to be human, also.

3. **Appeal to core values**. A benefit to getting to know your team members well is that you learn what they value most in every situation. Whatever you are trying to get them to comply with must be consistent with the core values significant to the person.

4. *Relinquish control* over how the idea or the assignment gets done. People are inspired when you share what you want and give them free rein to deliver the finished product or outcome. You must believe in the people around you.

5. *Offer new stretch opportunities*. We are excited to learn new skills, accomplish more goals, and achieve success in areas we never considered. Great leaders present challenges that stretch and allow their teams to evolve into something more than ever imagined.

Assume that everyone on your team wants to accomplish great things in life, including contributing to your organization. I encourage you to aspire to leave people better off than you found them. Allow the individual to determine what 'better off' looks like but commit to helping them define and reach meaningful success.

Chapter Summary:

This chapter highlights the differences between bosses and leaders regarding their focus on tasks and assignments. Bosses prioritize job performance and learning solely for the purpose of enhancing job-related skills. In contrast, leaders encourage individuals to deeply understand their core skills, talents, and competencies and align them with their life's purpose. Leaders genuinely care about the success of their team members, both personally and professionally. The chapter emphasizes the importance of understanding individual goals, inspiring team members to achieve their goals while completing assignments and providing opportunities for skill development and growth.

Recommended Action Plan:

1. Model inspiration: Be the best version of yourself and set an example that inspires others. Maintain a positive reputation, demonstrate good character, and exhibit consistent behavior. Your actions speak louder than words.

2. Share your journey: Be transparent about your own successes and failures and how you have overcome disappointments. Sharing your story humanizes you and encourages others to embrace their own humanity.

3. Appeal to core values: Take the time to understand the core values of your team members. Align your leadership approach and the organization's goals with their values, as this will inspire greater engagement and commitment.

4. Foster autonomy: Give team members autonomy and control over how they accomplish tasks and assignments. Believe in their abilities and trust them to deliver the desired outcomes. Providing freedom and trust inspires individuals to take ownership and excel.

5. Offer stretch opportunities: Create opportunities for team members to learn new skills, set ambitious goals, and achieve success in areas they may not have considered before. Encourage their growth and evolution by presenting challenges that expand their capabilities.

6. Assume greatness: Approach each team member with the belief that they have the potential to accomplish

great things, both within the organization and in life. Cultivate an environment that supports and nurtures individual aspirations.

7. Leave a positive impact: Strive to leave individuals better off than when you found them. Help team members define and reach their own versions of meaningful success. Support their personal growth and development, even if it means they eventually move on from the organization.

By implementing these actions, leaders can inspire and empower their team members to align their skills and goals with their life's purpose. This fosters a sense of fulfillment and engagement, resulting in improved performance and a positive work environment.

Create your personal 90-Day Action Plan:

1)

2)

3)

4)

5)

Empathy Isn't Profanity

Position #4:

> *Bosses believe emotions get in the way of doing business except when trying to manipulate and influence a sale.*
>
> *Leaders know that employee engagement increases when individuals know that people in the workplace care about them and their life's events.*

The workplace has become sterile and impersonal. Let us stop the insensitive and harsh tactics in business and care equally for the members of our organizations as we do for our clients and customers. No one is expecting business leaders to act as a Pastor or Priest. However, the COVID-19 pandemic, racial issues, and social unrest in the United States of America in 2020 proved that no one is exempt from suffering. Everyone has a day of despair. The recent hurt felt across the world rattles your very being and brings a level of disappointment that you cannot explain. I believe that more of our society has moved from apathy to degrees of sympathy and from sympathy to empathy.

Leaders understand that empathy is critical to your success. People have gone through a lot recently. You must bring the heart back into business. It is not as big of a stretch anymore unless you believe that some deserve misery while others should be exempt. I encourage you to grasp the complexity of empathy and apply it in your daily interactions with your teams. Stop being so focused on results and help others live again. It is okay that you empathize with others. You will not lose yourself in the process once you have a better understanding of what empathy is and how to use it.
Empathy, as defined by **'*Psychology Today*'** is:

> Empathy is the ability to recognize, understand, and share the thoughts and feelings of another person. Developing empathy is crucial for establishing relationships and behaving

compassionately. Empathy helps us cooperate with others, build friendships, make moral decisions, and intervene when we see others bullied. Humans begin to show signs of empathy in infancy, and the trait develops steadily through childhood and adolescence. Still, most people are likely to feel greater empathy for people like themselves and may feel less empathy for those outside their family, community, ethnicity, or race.[1]

You can increase your empathy by spending time with people outside of your circle. Build relationships with those who have different customs and practices. You experience life from many perspectives when you read literature by various authors, watch videos, movies, and explore music created by people of different cultures. Venture into unfamiliar cultures to gain insight and become more empathetic. Spend time reflecting on what you experienced, the similarities, and how the differences could enhance your approach.

There is a language to empathy. **Kate Miller-Wilson from YourDictionary.com** provides examples of empathy statements you can use when interacting with students/trainees, co-workers/employees, and customers.[2]

Empathy statements for students and trainees:
- It must be frustrating when students turn things in late. I'm sorry.
- I can see how hard you tried here.
- I know what it feels like to get a lousy grade.
- I'm sorry this is so discouraging right now.
- It sounds like you were doing the best you could, even though it was difficult.
- I've been there. Some school days are just really hard.
- I know it feels like no one understands, but I'm listening right now.
- It's perfectly normal to feel frustrated in a situation like this.
- I know you feel like giving up right now, and I'm glad you aren't.
- It has to be difficult to deal with this.

Empathy statements for co-workers and employees:

- I know you've put so much time and effort into this, and it must be frustrating to see the project shut down.
- Uncertainty is really hard.
- That has to be confusing and discouraging.
- If that happened to me, I would feel upset too.
- Times of change are hard, and it's totally normal that you're feeling anxious about this.
- I would be upset if someone talked to me that way too.
- I can hear your concern in your voice.
- You must feel like no one even listened to your idea.
- I know it isn't easy to deal with stuff like this, but you are handling it so well.
- It's been a difficult couple of weeks, hasn't it?

Empathy statements for customers:

- I understand how frustrating it must be to wait this long for your order.
- If I were in your position, I would be upset too.
- I'm so glad you contacted us about that; it's important that we get it fixed.
- I know you've spent a lot of time on this already.
- Your patience here has been so important.
- I know you have a lot of choices, so I want to make sure we meet your needs. Can you tell me more about what you're looking for?
- After all this, anyone would be frustrated.
- So, what I hear you saying is ...
- It makes total sense you would need some help with this.
- Our mistake has cost you a lot of time and money. Let me make it right.

Chapter Summary:

This chapter explores the difference between bosses and leaders when it comes to empathy in the workplace. Bosses tend to prioritize results and overlook the importance of empathy, while leaders understand the significance of empathy in building relationships and creating a compassionate work environment. The chapter emphasizes the need for leaders to embrace empathy, understand its definition and importance, and provides examples of empathy statements that can be used in interactions with students/trainees, co-workers/employees, and customers.

Recommended Action Plan:

1. Grasp the concept of empathy: Take the time to understand what empathy means and why it is crucial in the workplace. Recognize that empathy is about recognizing, understanding, and sharing the thoughts and feelings of others.

2. Expand your perspective: Seek out experiences, literature, videos, movies, and music from different cultures and perspectives. Engage with people outside of your usual circle to gain insights and broaden your understanding of different customs and practices.

3. Reflect on your experiences: After engaging with different cultures and perspectives, take time to reflect on what you have learned. Identify similarities and consider how differences can enhance your approach to interactions and relationships.

4. Use empathy statements: Familiarize yourself with empathy statements that can be used in various contexts, such as interactions with students/trainees, co-workers/employees, and customers. Practice incorporating these statements into

your conversations to demonstrate empathy and understanding.

5. Show empathy in student/trainee interactions: When interacting with students or trainees, acknowledge their frustrations, efforts, and difficulties. Let them know that you understand their challenges and offer support and encouragement.

6. Demonstrate empathy with co-workers/employees: Show empathy towards your co-workers and employees by acknowledging their feelings and concerns. Validate their experiences and provide reassurance during times of change or difficulty. Let them know that you understand their emotions and appreciate their efforts.

7. Display empathy with customers: When interacting with customers, empathize with their frustrations or concerns. Acknowledge the difficulties they have faced and express a genuine desire to help. Offer support, listen actively, and work towards resolving any issues or challenges they may be experiencing.

8. Cultivate a compassionate work environment: Lead by example and create a work environment that values empathy and care. Encourage open communication, active listening, and understanding among team members. Foster a culture where everyone feels heard, understood, and supported.

By incorporating empathy into your leadership approach, you can create a workplace environment that values the well-being and experiences of individuals. This will contribute to increased employee engagement, stronger relationships, and overall success for both individuals and the organization.

Create your personal 90-Day Action Plan:

1)

2)

3)

4)

5)

Not Less Than

Position #5:

Bosses see themselves as superior to those they are leading. They devalue anyone who shows any sign of weakness.

Leaders are confident in what they know and commit to becoming more intelligent every day. When someone needs help, a leader sees it as a learning opportunity for the individual and themselves.

Team members needing help does not mean that they are less than the person who understands the same topics. Don't we all have places with unknown answers or that we have not mastered? No one is perfect. No one is all-knowing. When training or coaching individuals, you must see the person as a valuable human being with skills, knowledge, and building experiences.

To prevent the "I think I am better than you because of your lack of knowledge syndrome," ask everyone to share something with the team they have mastered. You are developing an inventory of resources within the group. The "go-to individuals" are known for their areas of interest and expertise. No one should be exempt because it will stimulate team members to identify and build their skills and competencies in their most significant interest areas. Encourage increased direct interaction. More meaningful communication will foster better collaboration.

The truth is that no one can produce a quality product or service alone. There is too much to do from the birth of the vision to deliver to the ideal audience. Value and help the team become better together by modeling how powerful helping one another can be to the person and organization. You do not get to wear a 'superiority badge' because you have knowledge that others do not. People see your flaws just as clearly as they see your strength. Your team may be polite in not expressing your inadequacies but never think you can hide all your faults and failures. Some of your weaknesses are blind spots to you and visible to everyone else. The reality of your imperfections calls for a humble confidence in your strengths. Do not underestimate or downplay your expertise. Be grateful for your ability to perform at such a high level and willingly help others understand what you know. Do not be a know-it-all. Do not share unsolicited information. People will hate to see you coming if you boast and talk too much about you and what you know. Remember, you have nothing to prove to anyone. You can share knowledge and experience with any interested audience. Empower those requesting your help to complete their tasks and leave them with a desire to learn more. When those around you understand the passion you have for a topic, they will learn to value it also.

When sharing your expert knowledge, here are a few tips to keep in mind:

1. **Make sure you understand the question and the context**. Answer the specific question and only give examples, statistics, or more data if relevant for better understanding.

2. **Show how best to apply the knowledge** you share with examples like the scenario discussed.

3. **Check for understanding, and do not interrogate**. Trust the individual to own their learning process.

4. ***Provide a window of opportunity for the person to ask additional questions***. The timeframe and conditions for follow-up must be agreeable to both of you.

5. ***Share upfront how much time you can give to help***. Sharing your availability will help the individual better manage their time with you and take the training more seriously. You are not obligated to be available when the trainee decides they want to engage. Help the individual to be accountable for their learning.

6. ***Be creative and reshape the information*** so the trainee/employee/co-worker can connect to the concept and comprehend how to move forward. When you say the same thing the same way repeatedly, it does not help. A master of an idea or skill can present the data to an array of audiences.

7. ***Do not overcomplicate the matter***. Keep your explanation simple. If the subject is complex, break up the information to establish the proper foundation or basics before adding layers.

8. ***Desire to see the one you are helping succeed***. You are investing in the outcome. Show compassion and expect positive results. Let the person know you are hoping for their best.

Recognize that you have stepped into an opportunity to learn more about your field of expertise. Refuse to entertain the thought that you now get a chance to show off what you know. Strive to become more intelligent every day. You will learn from others and become more competent in what you understand by helping others. There are many resources available today. People can go anywhere for an answer. It is an honor when someone seeks your help. Treat this opportunity to share as a gift to you.

Chapter Summary:

This chapter highlights the contrasting attitudes of bosses and leaders when it comes to knowledge and helping others. Bosses view themselves as superior and devalue those who show weakness, while leaders are confident in their knowledge and see opportunities to help others as learning opportunities for both parties. The chapter emphasizes the importance of recognizing everyone's value, encouraging collaboration, and sharing expertise without arrogance or superiority.

Recommended Action Plan:

1. Embrace humility and confidence: Cultivate a mindset of humble confidence in your strengths and expertise. Recognize that no one is perfect or all-knowing and be open to learning from others. Appreciate your own abilities while acknowledging that you have weaknesses and areas for growth.

2. Build an inventory of resources: Encourage team members to share their areas of mastery and expertise with the team. Create a culture where individuals can openly discuss their skills and knowledge. This inventory of resources will facilitate collaboration and empower team members to develop their own skills in areas of interest.

3. Help others without superiority: When sharing your expert knowledge, avoid a superior or know-it-all attitude. Be grateful

for your abilities and willingly help others understand what you know. Share knowledge and experience with humility, without boasting or talking excessively about yourself.

4. Share knowledge effectively: When sharing knowledge, ensure that you understand the context and question at hand. Provide relevant examples and demonstrate how to apply the knowledge in practical scenarios. Check for understanding and create a space for individuals to ask additional questions.

5. Establish time availability: Communicate upfront how much time you can dedicate to helping others. Set clear expectations and boundaries regarding your availability. Encourage individuals to be accountable for their own learning and manage their time effectively.

6. Be creative and adaptable: Reshape information to connect with the individual's understanding and help them comprehend concepts. Avoid overcomplicating matters and keep explanations simple. Adapt your approach based on the audience and their level of knowledge.

7. Show compassion and desire for success: Approach helping others with a genuine desire to see them succeed. Invest in the outcome and demonstrate compassion. Let individuals know that you believe in their potential and expect positive results.

8. Embrace learning opportunities: Recognize that helping others is also an opportunity for personal growth. Refrain from showing off or seeking validation but strive to become more intelligent every day. Be open to learning from others and expanding your own competence in your field of expertise.

By implementing these actions, you can foster a collaborative and supportive work environment. By sharing knowledge without superiority, helping others effectively, and embracing opportunities for learning, you contribute to the growth and success of both individuals and the organization as a whole.

Create your personal 90-Day Action Plan:

1)

2)

3)

4)

5)

Lead and Solve with Integrity

The world is hungry for integral, strategic, influential, collaborative, and decisive leadership with a heart for everyone helping to fulfill the vision. No Bosses Allowed || Lead to Serve & Transform was birthed out of a desire to bring leadership to the level required to overcome these unprecedented times.

It sounds like this:

> *Leader: Here is WHAT I see, where we are going, when we need to get there, and the implications of we don't go.*

> *Team: Here are our recommendations for HOW we get there. We are equipped to quantify the costs, and risks, when we can deliver what you see verses what we can deliver in your desired timetable.*

Suppose you want your organization to sound more like this consistently. In that case, the *"Lead with Soul"* Community will help you develop stronger leaders and a higher-performing team.

I created *"Lead with Soul"* as a community to encourage leaders to continue to stretch, learn and perform with the highest level of excellence and consciousness. Every leader will enhance their balance for the profits and personal growth of their leaders and people. *"Lead with Soul"* also supports leaders at their lowest points, reminding them they will rise above every poor decision and adverse scenario stronger.

Many leaders seek a place where they can be themselves without fear of making a mistake. *"Lead with Soul"* is a community specifically designed as an engaging platform for all leaders, regardless of tenure. Leaders across multiple industries, sectors, and people groups share experiences in confidence, share challenges, and learn cutting-edge concepts in leadership. This network is created with all leadership styles in mind. If you are ready to maximize your experience, results and leave a legacy you are proud of, **check out to join Lead with Soul**. (https://buy.stripe.com/bIYcQ88P5fMq7yo7tj)

Bottom-line Counts

Position #6:

Bosses only care about increased revenue and profit. How they obtained the increase is not essential. Those who contributed to the growth are of little importance.

Leaders operate out of integrity and accuracy. Revenue, profit, and how success is obtained are equally important. Leaders are committed to the results, and everyone contributes to the results.

Phenomenal leaders prioritize people over their progress and personal gain but do not ignore the organization's profitability. You are in a position to fulfill the vision and the core objectives. Everything you do must tie back to why the organization exists. Balancing the purpose, the organization's needs and the growth of the teams is challenging. Lead to produce quality services and products that meet the needs of your clients/customers. Seek out people who will help you meet your objectives and goals. Here is the formula:

Vision Fulfilled = Goals/Objectives + Heart Engaged Partners

Great leaders achieve business goals and objectives through strategic planning involving your ideal audience and building an engaging culture. You must set the tone for the daily experiences. The culture is emphasized or ignored by how you and your supporting leadership teams execute the vision. There must be consistent messaging and attitudes throughout the enterprise to increase market share, growth, and expansion. The approaches may differ, but the intentional heart expressed through core values and objectives must remain the same and be reinforced often and broadly.

There is a cost to doing business. If you do not effectively manage the cost, everyone loses. You should always minimize expenses by spending wisely, even when serving and transforming your team into a more influential group. Creativity in producing better products/services ahead of the market shift is an admiral goal. Knowing when to remain stable and consistent is wisdom.

You cannot save, serve, or transform everyone. Everyone is not your assignment. This lesson was the best statement a colleague shared with me. When you get so hung up in trying to help the individuals around you, you lose yourself and focus on the main thing. Your primary responsibility is to create a healthy organization where individuals can thrive while fulfilling the vision. Know when to choose the welfare of the organization over an individual or team of individuals. All decisions will not be popular. You must be grounded to continue to steer the ship toward achieving excellence. Not everyone will choose to stay on the course. It is okay. Every twist, turn, acceleration, and slow down must be successfully responded to by everyone involved at the time of the change.

When you are executing the hard decisions, acknowledge the psychological impact on you as the leader. Would you please not ignore it or minimize it? The effects are real. You do not want to become brutal and insensitive simply because you are trying to move past a tough choice. Deal with it appropriately so you can still serve and transform those remaining to the best of your ability. The truth is that everyone is impacted when the survival of the organization takes precedence. Your response will make a difference in how the organization responds to the situation. It truly is a delicate and critical balance. Please do not approach the problem coldly or callously.

Be brave enough to stand by your decisions regardless of the backlash. Likely, someone within the team will not agree, voice their disagreement, and lose a level of trust and respect. Some will never understand until they walk in your shoes and must confront the same circumstances you had to address. Expect it. Plan your response considering how you would like the rest of the organization to move forward with you. Acknowledge the severity of the situation where required and set the direction by inspiring every person involved.

Speak from their frame of reference. What is in it for the team members and the bigger picture will inspire them to continue the journey with you despite the unfortunate losses recently suffered. Give people space and defined time to adjust to the change. You do not have to announce that they only have 60 or 90 days to adjust. You will set the pace via your actions and language. Navigate the transition through your leadership in how you release communications, what you say, and implement the changes.

Chapter Summary:

This chapter emphasizes the contrasting perspectives of bosses and leaders when it comes to prioritizing revenue and profit versus valuing people and integrity. Bosses focus solely on increasing revenue and profit without considering the means by which they are obtained or valuing those who contribute to the growth. In contrast, leaders operate with integrity, recognizing the equal importance of revenue, profit, and how success is achieved. Phenomenal leaders prioritize people and engage their hearts while still achieving business goals and objectives. They set the tone for the organization's culture, manage costs effectively, make tough decisions when necessary, and navigate transitions with empathy and clarity.

Recommended Action Plan:

1. Connect with the organization's purpose: Ensure that your actions and decisions tie back to the organization's vision and core objectives. Focus on producing quality products and services that meet the needs of your clients/customers while aligning with the organization's mission.

2. Build an engaging culture: Set the tone for the organization's daily experiences by fostering an engaging culture. Align messaging and attitudes across the enterprise, emphasizing core values and objectives. Reinforce the culture often and consistently to drive market share, growth, and expansion.

3. Manage costs wisely: Minimize expenses by spending wisely, even when investing in transforming and developing your team. Seek creative ways to improve products and services ahead of the market shift while knowing when stability and consistency are essential.

4. Make tough decisions for the welfare of the organization: Recognize that not everyone can be saved, served, or transformed. Focus on creating a healthy organization where individuals can thrive while fulfilling their vision. Be prepared to make decisions that prioritize the welfare of the organization over individual or team needs, understanding that not every decision will be popular.

5. Acknowledge the psychological impact: Recognize the psychological impact of executing hard decisions as a leader. Do not ignore or minimize it. Deal with the impact appropriately to maintain empathy and sensitivity while still serving and transforming the remaining individuals to the best of your ability.

6. Stand by your decisions: Be brave enough to stand by your decisions, even in the face of backlash or

disagreement. Understand that not everyone will understand or agree until they are in your shoes. Plan your response to maintain trust and respect and inspire the rest of the organization to move forward with you.

7. Speak from their frame of reference: When communicating changes or transitions, speak from the frame of reference of the team members and the bigger picture. Emphasize what is in it for them and how the organization will continue its journey despite recent losses. Give people space and defined time to adjust, and set the pace through your actions, language, and implementation of changes.

By following this action plan, leaders can strike a delicate balance between revenue, profit, and valuing people. They can effectively manage tough decisions, navigate transitions with empathy, and inspire the organization to move forward toward success.

Create your personal 90-Day Action Plan:
1)

2)

3)

4)

5)

Ownership Mentality

Position #7:

Bosses take ownership until something goes wrong. When there is a problem, they look for someone and something to blame.

Leaders exemplify and encourage their teams to own their roles and responsibilities regardless of whether the results are favorable.

Every person in every organization has a title for the job they hold. However, we store specific titles in high esteem because they represent power and privilege. There is no insignificant role in an organization. Think about it. You took the time to develop a description and requirements for each position. There is a salary or hourly wage allocated for the individual hired. In some cases, there are benefits also available. The above facts cause you to stop and think that if you have a need you are actively seeking to fill, why do you view any position as insignificant?

How do you make sure everyone sees their role as significant and owns their role? Taking accountability for achieving successful outcomes is the responsibility of everyone, not just the "owner" or senior leadership. It is better to be an expert with integrity, accuracy, timeliness, and consistency to contribute to a well-run organization. Oh yes, your performance matters to everyone. Remember, you would not have created the position and brought individuals onto the team if there was no essential need.

Throughout the organization, creating an ownership mentality is every leader's responsibility, starting with the one at the very top leading by example. Create an action plan or roadmap with the details you care about to ensure that everyone moves in the same direction on the same page. Delegate and empower those assigned to deliver the expected outcome. Communicate any changes to the plan or influences to the plan as soon as possible. Encourage direct communication between teams who are dependent on one another to complete the assignment successfully. Set up deliberate and frequent touchpoints to confirm that everyone is free of obstacles. Encourage groups to share new developments discovered to assess the impact to quality, timing, the scope of what is delivered, and whom, risks, and cost. Give safe space for mistakes and recovery. Reward and celebrate progress along the way.

Some team members will not act like owners, which does not mean that they are not capable. Never forget that everyone takes ownership of something in their lives. When you are not afraid of making the wrong decision, you take ownership. Chastisement and micro-managing shut down ownership. Hosting debriefing or retrospective or reflective conversations allows individuals to own mistakes and solutions for improved approaches in the future as everyone shares lessons learned. Would you please not let finger-pointing take place? Allow the team members to hold their accountability, responsibility, and areas for improvement, increasing ownership among the entire team and organization. Allow the weight of the errors without pouring salt into the wounds. Everyone should be supportive as individuals take ownership and consider different and better ways of handling scenarios. Everyone will have their turn in the seat of "not quite making it." Encourage as you would want to be encouraged when it is your turn.

Chapter Summary:

This chapter highlights the contrasting behavior of bosses who shift blame when problems arise and leaders who exemplify and encourage ownership within their teams. It emphasizes the significance of every role within an organization and the need for accountability and responsibility from all team members, regardless of their title or position. Leaders foster an ownership mentality throughout the organization, starting from the top, by leading by example, creating action plans, empowering individuals, promoting direct communication, and providing a safe space for mistakes and learning. They discourage finger-pointing and instead encourage individuals to take ownership of their mistakes, solutions, and areas for improvement.

Recommended Action Plan:

1. Recognize the significance of every role: Acknowledge that every position within the organization has value and purpose. Avoid viewing any role as insignificant and instead appreciate the contributions each team member makes.

2. Lead by example: Demonstrate ownership by taking responsibility for your actions, decisions, and outcomes. Show accountability and integrity in your own role to set a positive example for others to follow.

3. Create an action plan and roadmap: Develop a clear plan and share it with the team, ensuring that everyone understands the expectations, goals, and desired

outcomes. Provide the necessary resources and support to enable individuals to deliver the expected results.

4. Delegate and empower: Delegate tasks and responsibilities to individuals, empowering them to take ownership of their assigned roles. Trust their capabilities and provide the necessary autonomy to make decisions and execute their tasks effectively.

5. Foster direct communication: Encourage open and direct communication among teams that are interdependent and rely on one another for successful outcomes. Facilitate regular touchpoints and meetings to ensure alignment, address any challenges or obstacles, and promote collaboration.

6. Embrace mistakes and learning: Create a culture that accepts and learns from mistakes. Encourage individuals to take ownership of their mistakes and contribute to finding solutions and improved approaches. Conduct debriefing or retrospective conversations to share lessons learned and foster continuous improvement.

7. Discourage finger-pointing: Avoid blaming individuals when problems arise. Instead, foster an environment where team members hold themselves accountable and take ownership of their actions and areas for improvement. Encourage support and constructive feedback rather than criticism.

8. Provide encouragement and support: Celebrate progress and achievements along the way to motivate and inspire individuals. Offer support and encouragement to team members as they navigate

challenges and take ownership of their responsibilities. Create a positive and supportive environment.

By implementing this action plan, leaders can cultivate an ownership mentality throughout the organization. They can foster accountability, responsibility, and continuous improvement while discouraging blame and finger-pointing. Encouraging ownership will lead to a more engaged and empowered team that takes pride in their work and contributes to the overall success of the organization.

Create your personal 90-Day Action Plan:
1)

2)

3)

4)

5)

Color It Us

Position #8:

> Bosses expect people to work hard so the boss can look good.
>
> The accomplishments of their teams do not threaten leaders. Leaders gracefully receive acknowledgments of their success and outwardly celebrate those who helped them.

Give credit where credit is due. Do you have difficulty acknowledging the contributions of others? There are numerous reasons why leaders neglect to recognize the person(s) who made the difference between success or failure on any given assignment. Nevertheless, not promoting key contributors is damaging to the individual's morale, diminishing the team's effectiveness, creativity, and ingenuity. Why should anyone risk failure if you take all the credit or a person's efforts are watered down with a broad stroke as teamwork?

Great leaders say thank you often. Appreciating an individual is far more critical than simply acknowledging their work. When you are focused on achieving rather than enjoying those on the journey with you, you take people for granted, assuming every person must be present and perform well. While active engagement is a requirement of maintaining employment, the basic assumption is that everyone will complete their assignments. How a person completes the tasks given makes all the difference in the world. Move beyond thinking that anyone owes you or must do a job or else. Statements such as, "You are here to do a job, so just get it done," are demeaning and degrading, lowering the person in value, and social position, discrediting, shaming, dishonoring, humiliating, and undermining. There is no motivation to explore quality solutions that allow the organization to step above its competition when you ignore a person's efforts. Everyone contributes to the level of success the organization gains. You will only go as far as the sum of your entire team allows. Increase your success ratio by increasing the engagement of your entire organization by appreciating even the smallest gestures that make the work easier.

Public acknowledgment is enormous even in the minds of those who say they would like to remain anonymous. Below are suggestions on how to make known the achievements of individuals.

Along the journey to your goal, here are suggested ways to give acknowledgment:

1. Thank the team for reaching specific milestones that help you get closer to the end.
2. Give praise to the one who comes up with a perspective during a conversation that refreshes and reignites the team's potential to reach a better solution.
3. Let individuals know you appreciate them for doing their assignments well.

4. Express the benefits realized all because completing assignments completed on time and the level of quality expected or exceeded expectations.
5. When introducing team members to others, share their role and position and how critical they are to the team often. The more people hear how you value them to others, the more they will sacrifice to help you win.
6. Allow grace to team members who may have had a moment of less favorable performance. Team members should seek ways to help fill in the gaps when someone is having a bad day. Acknowledge when someone picks up the slack to help another member of the team.
7. Appreciate it when someone keeps you updated on their statuses in advance so you can shift resources or communicate changes in delivery time before the deadline.

Below are suggestions for celebrations and appreciation once you reach the goal:

1. Personally, thank those who contributed.
2. If a team was involved, thank the entire team for the specific ways they worked well together.
3. When your leader or people outside your team celebrate you for the accomplishment, quickly share that you had a group of folks working with you contributing daily to the successful outcome.
4. Present the results leading with your appreciation for the team's hard work and any individual critical acknowledgments.
5. Be specific when saying thank you. Sharing why you appreciate a team or individual reinforces that

behavior and competency. Everyone will know you understand the essential details that made a difference.

6. Verbalize and send notes of thanks in writing, copying your leadership and other leaders who directly influence the trajectory of the career, rewards, and financial gains of everyone who contributed to the results.

7. Remember, no act is too small. Without the finite detail, the level of success experienced would not be possible.

8. Never be tempted to take the credit that belongs to anyone else. Yes, you are the leader and provide direction. You are supposed to assist the individual or team with navigating successfully. It speaks to your integrity when you quickly direct accolades to the person(s) deserving of them.

I hear the hurt of many who worked hard to keep a project or department running, and the leader overseeing the effort, who never really contributes, gets all the public acknowledgment. Everyone involved, directly and indirectly, may not know the details of how much anyone helped. Still, they always know who did not help. You do not get to take credit because this person or team reports to you on an organization chart. Readily acknowledge the success of those who achieved the outcome.

Chapter Summary:

This chapter highlights the negative behavior of bosses who take credit for the work of their teams and fail to acknowledge their contributions. In contrast, great leaders prioritize giving credit where credit is due and celebrate the success of their team members. Recognizing the efforts of individuals is crucial for boosting morale, enhancing team effectiveness, and fostering creativity and innovation. Leaders who appreciate and acknowledge their team members create a more engaged and motivated workforce. The chapter provides suggestions for giving acknowledgment and celebrating achievements as a way to show gratitude and reinforce positive behaviors.

Recommended Action Plan:

1. Value every contribution: Recognize the importance of every team member's role and the impact they have on the organization's success. Avoid dismissing or diminishing anyone's efforts, regardless of their position or responsibilities.

2. Say thank you often: Express appreciation regularly to individuals and the entire team for their contributions, milestones reached, and successful outcomes. Foster a culture of gratitude and recognition.

3. Acknowledge specific achievements: Be specific when expressing appreciation to individuals or the team. Highlight the ways in which their work has made a difference and contributed to the overall success of the organization.

4. Publicly acknowledge contributions: Make efforts to publicly recognize individuals' achievements and their role in reaching goals. Share their accomplishments with others, both within and outside the organization.

5. Celebrate as a team: When goals are achieved, celebrate collectively as a team. Thank the entire team for their collaboration, teamwork, and collective efforts

in achieving the desired outcomes. Emphasize the importance of working together to accomplish success.

6. Communicate contributions to others: Introduce team members to others, highlighting their roles and positions and how their contributions are critical to the team's success. Reinforce their value and the impact they have on the organization.

7. Show grace and support: Acknowledge when team members may be having a challenging day or moment and appreciate it when others step in to help. Foster a supportive environment where team members support one another and fill in the gaps when needed.

8. Express gratitude in writing: Along with verbal appreciation, send written notes of thanks to individuals and the team, copying relevant leaders who can influence career growth, rewards, and financial gains. Be specific in expressing gratitude and highlight the details that made a difference.

9. Redirect accolades to deserving individuals: As the leader, quickly direct acknowledgments and accolades to the individuals or teams who deserve them. Avoid taking credit for others' work and openly recognize those who contributed to the successful outcomes.

By implementing this action plan, leaders can cultivate a culture of appreciation and recognition within the organization. They can create an environment where individuals feel valued, motivated, and acknowledged for their contributions. Celebrating achievements and giving credit where it is due fosters a positive work atmosphere, enhances teamwork, and reinforces a sense of ownership and pride among team members.

Create your personal 90-Day Action Plan:

1)

2)

3)

4)

5)

We See It

Position #9:

Bosses create and share all the details of every vision. Everything must be to their specifications.

Leaders want their teams to enhance their vision. Leaders appreciate how collaboration builds better products and services.

What makes you different is the vision for your organization.
- What do you see for your organization?
- How will you make an impact in this industry?
- Why are you here currently?
- Who will care that you exist?

The questions asked above are sample questions. Answer such questions often to create and increase momentum. Your entire organization must own the vision. You cannot obtain what you cannot see. Influence the outcome by helping members of your team fully understand where you are headed and why. Every member will be able to share confidently then what the organization is doing and why.

Vision Casting is the tool used to share and reinforce an organization's future, why, and how you plan to get to the desired state. Those aligned with you to move the vision to reality will expand the idea and make it an everyday occurrence. The collaboration will bring a huge relief to the visionary. Your perspective as a visionary leader is limited. No one knows everything. The details come from the views, experiences, knowledge, and skills of everyone who signed up to help you fulfill the vision. Share as much as you can see and allow others to help you move towards the goal.

Be open to your team filling in the blanks beyond what you see. However, make sure every idea presented resonates with you as a great addition. There is a delicate balance between navigating through new and uncomfortable stretches of your imagination vs. ideas taking you off your desired path. Be honest with yourself and your confidants as you work through the challenges to achieving more than what you alone could imagine. Avoid pitfalls and undesired sidebars that you never intended. Seek to grow along the journey but do not let anyone force you down an unsettling path. Honor your intentions throughout the process.

Take the following steps to start vision casting:

1. Be clear on your vision by writing it down in as many details as possible.
2. Organize the vision so it is digestible to every member and team in your organization. Remember, people are constantly asking, "What's in it for me?" Help them see where they fit in, helping to bring the vision to reality.
3. Share the vision as broadly as possible. Create a version of what you want to share with your internal teams, vendors, customers, clients, investors, family and friends, industry, and the community where you operate. Everyone should know the benefits of you being here now and in this specific location(s).
4. Share and reinforce the vision in writing, verbally, through images, actions, and behaviors. Listen and watch how others state and act on the idea.
5. Schedule a specific time during the year to share what you see for the months ahead.

6. Schedule times throughout the year to share accomplishments toward the vision.
7. Immediately share updates to the vision. Changes and additions will impact how people are responding to the idea today. Plans may need to be adjusted as members of your teams expand and implement the vision. Let them know early and often when you see more so, they can incorporate the additions.
8. Look for opportunities throughout the day to share how people take ties back to the vision. If an action does not support the concept directly or indirectly, it should be questioned. Everything must tie back to the idea and core values established.

The notion of "When I see it, I'll believe it" is authentic. Your goal is to help the entire organization believe that they look to help others feel what you are doing, why, and how.

Chapter Summary:

This chapter emphasizes the difference between bosses who dictate every detail of a vision and leaders who encourage collaboration and enhancement of the vision by their teams. Leaders understand the power of shared vision and collaboration in building better products and services. The chapter encourages leaders to clearly define their vision, involve the entire organization in understanding and owning the vision, and be open to ideas and contributions from team members. It provides steps for vision casting and effective communication to ensure alignment and progress toward the desired future.

Recommended Action Plan:

1. Define and document your vision: Clearly articulate your vision in detail, outlining what you see for your organization, how you plan to make an impact, and why you exist. Write it down to have a tangible reference point.

2. Organize the vision for clarity: Organize your vision in a way that is easily understandable and relatable for every member and team in your organization. Help individuals see where they fit into the vision and how their contributions contribute to its realization.

3. Share the vision broadly: Develop different versions of the vision tailored to different audiences, such as internal teams, vendors, customers, investors, and the community. Communicate the benefits of your organization's presence and operations to each stakeholder group.

4. Reinforce the vision consistently: Communicate the vision through various channels, including written documents, verbal communication, visual representations, and your actions and behaviors. Continuously reinforce the vision in your interactions with others. Pay attention to how others understand and interpret the vision.

5. Schedule regular vision updates: Set specific times throughout the year to share updates and progress towards the vision. Use these opportunities to celebrate accomplishments, address challenges, and realign strategies if needed.

6. Share immediate updates: If there are changes or additions to the vision, communicate them promptly. Keep your teams informed and engaged by sharing any updates that may impact their work or implementation of the vision.

7. Connect actions to the vision: Look for opportunities throughout the day to demonstrate how people's actions align with the vision. If an action does not support the vision or its core values, question its relevance and discuss ways to realign it with the overall vision.

8. Foster collaboration and contribution: Encourage team members to contribute their ideas and perspectives to enhance the vision. Be open to filling in the gaps beyond your own perspective while ensuring that any additions resonate with the overall vision and goals.

9. Believe in and embody the vision: Lead by example and fully embody the vision yourself. Show your belief in the vision and inspire others to believe in it too. Be passionate, consistent, and committed to the vision, reinforcing its importance and impact.

By implementing this action plan, leaders can effectively cast and communicate their vision, engage their teams, and foster a sense of ownership and collaboration. A shared vision creates alignment, boosts motivation, and empowers individuals to contribute their ideas and efforts toward the organization's success.

Create your personal 90-Day Action Plan:

1)

2)

3)

4)

5)

Power of Your Presence

Position #10:

Bosses show up when dignitaries visit when there is a problem or an important event that allows them to flaunt their power.

Leaders are often visible to provide support, eliminate obstacles, and celebrate achievements.

You must be accessible, so the teams know you know what they are doing. Your teams expect to get frequent updates and insight from you. Most importantly, your presence demonstrates how much you care about the vision. There is a difference between micromanaging and showing interest in the work and those completing the work. Bosses say, "I just want the work done." "I don't care how it gets done; just do it." Yes, you want the objectives met; however, how you meet them is equally important. Set the climate of how the organization moves towards your goals. You must be present in the game throughout the entire process.

Think about the NFL or NBA. The goals are to become the number one franchise with the champion team. The owners do not hire people to fill the organization's roles and then go off, ignoring the day-to-day or week-to-week activities. League owners invest approximately $15,000 to $30,000 per football game in skyboxes to have the best vantage point to watch the games. The owners are present, watching the game, entertaining investors and key stakeholders. They are aware of who is making the plays and who contributes.

Your organization probably does not have skyboxes for you to sit to observe the day-to-day activities. You can, however, visit teams and chat with individuals throughout the day to gain greater awareness of the successes and challenges. Request to be included in the distribution of meetings held by the team so you can attend and listen in to increase your awareness and offer support, if appropriate. No one should ever say that they do not know the owner or most senior leader(s). Allow the members of your organization to get to know you. Show up often so they have access to you.

Access also includes giving your undivided attention. Listen more than you speak when making yourself available. You are there in the moment to learn about matters to the team. As they share, begin to ask yourself how you could help eliminate roadblocks. Before you act, ask the group or individual you are working with, "How can I help?". Your assumptions on how to help fix the issues may not be what the team needs. Work with them to agree on where you can be most helpful and by when. Your willingness to help is excellent, but if you cannot assist for weeks ahead, it will not be beneficial at all.

Be intentional in learning the names of those involved and their skills. You are not there to simply make an appearance. Your presence allows people to connect and partner with you to fulfill the vision.

Chapter Summary:

This chapter highlights the difference between bosses who only show up for high-profile events or when there are problems and leaders who are consistently visible to provide support, eliminate obstacles, and celebrate achievements. Leaders understand the importance of accessibility, frequent updates, and showing genuine interest in the work and the people completing it. They set the climate for the organization by being present throughout the entire process and demonstrating their care for the vision.

Recommended Action Plan:

1. Be consistently present: Make an effort to be visible and accessible to your teams on a regular basis. Show up for team meetings, visit workspaces, and engage in conversations with individuals throughout the day. Be present to gain awareness of the successes and challenges within the organization.

2. Request inclusion in team meetings: Ask to be included in meetings held by different teams to increase your awareness of their work and offer support if appropriate. This demonstrates your interest and commitment to understanding the details of the organization's operations.

3. Foster personal connections: Take the time to learn the names of team members and their respective skills. Make an effort to connect with individuals on a personal level to build relationships and partnerships. Show genuine interest in their work and contributions.

4. Listen actively: When you make yourself available, prioritize active listening. Allow team members to share their perspectives, challenges, and ideas. Listen more than you speak and ask open-ended questions

to deepen your understanding. Resist the urge to jump to conclusions or provide immediate solutions.

5. Ask, "How can I help?": Before taking action or offering solutions, ask the team or individual how you can best assist them. Collaborate on identifying roadblocks and finding solutions together. Be open to their input and suggestions on where your support would be most beneficial.

6. Give undivided attention: When you are present with your teams, give them your undivided attention. Avoid distractions and focus on the matters at hand. Show respect for their time and contributions by actively engaging in discussions and providing thoughtful input.

7. Be mindful of your availability: Be realistic about your availability and ability to assist. If you cannot offer immediate help or support, communicate this openly and work with the team to establish a suitable timeline. Your willingness to help is important, but it should align with their needs and timelines.

8. Celebrate achievements: In addition to providing support and eliminating obstacles, make it a point to celebrate achievements and milestones. Recognize and appreciate the efforts and contributions of individuals and teams. Publicly acknowledge their successes to foster a positive and motivating work environment.

By implementing these actions, leaders can establish a visible and supportive presence within their organization. Being accessible, engaged, and genuinely interested in the work and the people involved cultivates a culture of collaboration, accountability, and commitment to the shared vision.

Create your personal 90-Day Action Plan:
1)

2)

3)

4)

5)

Flexing Leadership Style

Position #11:

Bosses expect everything to adapt to their communication preferences.

Leaders know that full engagement requires different approaches to interacting with individuals and teams to resolve issues, meet objectives and mitigate risks.

Servant/transformational leadership works in all types and sizes of organizations. While supporting the development of an individual, you will inspire them to complete the goals and objectives that enable the organization to realize the vision. Development and inspiration go hand in hand. Be sure to invest in the growth and nurturing of those same skills to further your cause. Growth companies love servant/transformational leaders because they push every individual to reach their potential while recognizing that individuals have different learning curves.

Various circumstances require agility in your approach to leadership. Shifting appropriately with the opportunities and challenges supports the development and transformation of your team by increasing their ability to flex also. You must switch to a different leadership style to significantly influence the situation. There are many different approaches. Below is a list of leadership styles I believe complement the goals of a servant/transformational leader. I encourage you to add to your leadership toolkit to support your primary leadership style.

Strategic: As you lead people out of their comfort zone into their greater self, it is essential to align with the organization's strategic plans. Lead individuals to take risks in areas that will benefit their personal growth and the organization's current objectives. You will create a win-win scenario. Assignments aligned with key performance indicators carry a greater weight and provide more visibility.

Democracy: When you desire to get the broadest engagement, gather insight to gain agreement from the entire team. Everyone may not agree 100%. However, agree to disagree and move forward. Support the team in the majority's recommendation.

Diplomatic: There are times when you and your team will not fulfill a request or meet a timeline. Always look to create and maintain strong relationships. It is vital in cases where you must deliver less favorable news that you do so that leaders understand your reasoning and agree with your decision.

Transactional: Workplaces highly regulated usually employ transactional leadership. There are quotas or rules you must have the team follow as the products and services are delivered. There is a lot less collaboration. This leadership style is most effective when you need everyone to shift immediately to meet a new deadline or become compliant. Everyone must complete the task as directed in the timeframe given.

Laisse-Faire: It is advantageous to step back and empower your team to work out how to achieve their objectives on their own. You may want to use this leadership style temporarily and only after providing your organization with strategic direction and coaching through servant/transformational leading. You encourage more innovation, risk-taking, and self-management when you shift to laisse-faire leading.

Chapter Summary:

This chapter discusses the difference between bosses who expect everything to adapt to their communication preferences and leaders who understand the importance of adapting their communication approaches to engage individuals and teams effectively. Servant/transformational leadership recognizes the need for different leadership styles to resolve issues, meet objectives, and mitigate risks. It emphasizes the development and inspiration of individuals while accommodating their diverse learning curves.

Recommended Action Plan:

1. Embrace agility: Recognize that different situations call for different leadership approaches. Be agile and flexible in your leadership style, adapting to the opportunities and challenges that arise. Understand that your team's development and transformation require you to be versatile as well.

2. Expand your leadership toolkit: Add additional leadership styles to complement your primary servant/transformational leadership approach. Consider incorporating the following styles:

- Strategic leadership: Align individual goals and assignments with the organization's strategic plans. Encourage individuals to take risks in areas that benefit their growth and contribute to current objectives. Create a win-win scenario where personal growth aligns with key performance indicators.

- Democratic leadership: Seek broad engagement and gather input from the entire team. Strive for consensus while acknowledging that not everyone may fully agree. Support the team in moving forward, even if there are differing viewpoints.

- Diplomatic leadership: Maintain strong relationships while delivering less favorable news or facing challenges. Ensure leaders understand your reasoning and decision-making process, fostering understanding and agreement.

- Transactional leadership: Employ this style in highly regulated workplaces with specific quotas or rules. Use it when immediate shifts are required to meet deadlines or compliance requirements. Focus on task completion and adherence to directives.

- Laissez-faire leadership: Empower your team to work autonomously and find their own ways to achieve objectives. Use this style selectively, providing strategic direction and coaching through servant/transformational leadership. Encourage innovation, risk-taking, and self-management.

3. Assess the situation: Evaluate each situation to determine the most appropriate leadership style to employ. Consider the goals, the nature of the task or challenge, and the characteristics of your team. Use your judgment to determine which style will best support the desired outcomes.

4. Continuously develop your leadership skills: Invest in your own growth and development as a leader. Seek opportunities to enhance your understanding of different leadership styles and how they can be applied effectively. Attend leadership development programs, read relevant books, and engage in self-reflection to refine your leadership approach.

5. Communicate and explain decisions: Regardless of the leadership style you employ, maintain open and transparent communication with your team. Clearly explain the reasoning behind your decisions and ensure leaders understand and agree with them. Strengthen relationships and foster understanding through effective communication.

By incorporating these actions into your leadership approach, you can enhance your effectiveness as a leader. Adapting your communication styles and leadership approaches based on the situation and needs of your team will promote engagement, development, and overall success in achieving organizational objectives.

Create your personal 90-Day Action Plan:

1)

2)

3)

4)

5)

Stop Flying Solo

Position #12:

> *Bosses hold everything close to their chest, sharing little information with their teams. As a result, they carry a great level of frustration and the full weight of challenges.*

> *Leaders encourage collaboration and create think tanks so the creativity and outcomes are shared across the team, maintaining engagement.*

You run the risk of fatigue and burnout due to significant demands when you fly solo. Consistently producing results, keeping your organization visible to customers and key stakeholders by releasing new quality products and services is taxing. Your goal is to be at the right place, at the right time, doing the right thing, in the right way, with the right people is the game's objective. There is one stipulation. You cannot lead alone and maintain the proper balance. Connecting with leaders committed to strengthening the field of leaders ensures increased performance and a place to test ideas and grow.

Teams are suffering under the leadership of individuals that have been stretched beyond the point of self-recovery. You may be trying to hold on and keep your business or department afloat. You have entirely run out of steam and have nowhere to turn for support or reinforcement. Teams are victims of leaders who are not professionally trained. Left to your own devices, you will not reach the level of maturity in leadership required to succeed in every industry.

The Lead With Soul Community gives you access to individuals equipped to help you master the behaviors successful leaders do every day. The information available to you is the culminated wisdom of multiple careers in leadership across different sectors.

Here are some lessons you can all learn from the Northern Bald Ibis.

- Fly with those headed in the same direction.
- Build a team that allows you to switch leadership positions so you can regain your energy.
- Create an upstream flow that gives a free lift to those following you easy access to help the team move forward.
- Get in the most favorable position and move at your most optimal pace to reach your destination.
- Increase your ability to quickly adjust your behavior to respond to what comes at you appropriately.
- Watch those ahead of you, do what they do and respond to positive feedback.
- Invest in your learning while helping your peers on the same path.

Great leaders see the potential and encourage individuals to reach what seems to be impossible. The people and the place are your focus instead of personal gain. You are honest, courageous, humble, integral, and invest time in people. You are also clear, decisive, humble, transparent, watchful, sensitive to your surroundings, and passionate.

On the contrary, bosses who want to be the boss tend to be self-focused, assertive, domineering, authoritative, in charge, overbearing, and arrogant. Members of your team are not invited to contribute to strategic plans or develop ideas.

Being a leader can be lonely, challenging, overwhelming, and frustrating, which is why I created the *"Lead With Soul" Community*. __*We are a group*__ of influential leaders committed to changing how leadership looks, sounds, and leaves people feeling. We strategically target spaces to shift leaders' thoughts at all levels independent of the industry segment. It is time to create a leadership culture that attracts and not repels.

As a member of *"Lead With Soul,"* you are joining an inspiring community holding each member accountable to maintain our core values and authenticity. You will encounter various leadership styles as you collaborate, share strategies, and broaden your perspective through networking. Leaders who lead and solve with integrity need support in a world that appears to be more cutthroat than kind. We will change that dynamic, showing everyone that doing what's right still rules.

Membership Benefits Include:
- Easily access support when you need it.
- Build successful relationships.
- Be a recognized influential voice.
- Master the things successful leaders do every day.
- Being featured in our magazine, "*The Diplomat Chronicles.*"
- Write & Submit Articles for our magazine, "*The Diplomat Chronicles.*"

- Discount on chapters for future Anthology
- Discounts on Events, Courses & Retreats
- Access to Private Facebook group
- Live Challenge discussions
- Insight to overcome hurdles.
- Celebrations as you progress.
- Special offerings for members of our community
- Opportunities for 1-on-1 Conversations with Yvette

Each month you will get a Bundle of Power Plays. – exclusive content to help you reach your goals. There are LIVE monthly group Power Chats to explore solutions to your challenges. You will network with those who excel as leaders and significantly impact various industries. Power exists in every relationship, in every moment on multiple levels. The question is not IF power exists; the questions are:

- Are you conscious of your power?
- Do you explore your power?
- Are you using your power to heal?

I invite you to lock in your monthly subscription at **$97.00 USD**. I look forward to transforming leadership together. *"Lead with Soul"* is a movement. **Check out to join** *Lead With Soul* or SCAN the QR Code.

Chapter Summary:

This chapter highlights the difference between bosses who hold information close and share little with their teams, leading to frustrations and a heavy burden, and leaders who encourage collaboration, create think tanks, and share creativity and outcomes across the team. It emphasizes the importance of connecting with other leaders and seeking support to avoid fatigue and burnout. The chapter also introduces the *Lead With Soul Community* as a resource for accessing wisdom and support from experienced leaders.

Recommended Action Plan:

1. Recognize the limitations of flying solo: Understand that leading alone can lead to fatigue and burnout. Acknowledge the significant demands of consistently producing results and maintaining visibility for your organization. Embrace the idea that you cannot lead alone and maintain a proper balance.

2. Connect with other leaders: Seek out leaders who are committed to strengthening the field of leaders. Look for opportunities to join communities, networks, or groups where you can connect with like-minded individuals. Engage in conversations, share experiences, and learn from one another.

3. Seek support and reinforcement: Don't be afraid to ask for support and seek reinforcement when needed. Share your challenges and frustrations with trusted peers or mentors who can provide guidance and encouragement. Embrace the idea that seeking help is a sign of strength, not weakness.

4. Join the *Lead With Soul Community*: Explore the resources and opportunities provided by the *Lead With Soul Community*. Access the wisdom and expertise of

leaders across different sectors who can help you master the behaviors of successful leaders. Take advantage of the community's knowledge and support to enhance your leadership skills.

5. Learn from the Northern Bald Ibis: Reflect on the lessons from the Northern Bald Ibis and apply them to your leadership approach. Fly with those who share the same direction, build a team that allows for leadership rotation to regain energy, create an upstream flow to support team progress, find the most favorable position and pace, be adaptable and responsive, learn from those ahead of you, and invest in your learning while supporting your peers.

6. Embrace the qualities of a great leader: Focus on the people and the organization rather than personal gain. Be honest, courageous, humble, and invest time in people. Practice clarity, decisiveness, humility, transparency, vigilance, sensitivity to your surroundings, and passion in your leadership approach.

7. Foster collaboration and inclusivity: Encourage team members to contribute to strategic plans and idea development. Create a culture that values diverse perspectives and encourages everyone to participate in shaping the organization's direction. Emphasize the importance of collaboration and inclusivity to enhance creativity and outcomes.

By following this action plan, you can transition from being a boss to becoming a leader who fosters collaboration, seeks support, and embodies the qualities of a great leader.

Embracing the Lead With Soul Community and learning from the lessons provided will further enhance your leadership journey.

Create your personal 90- Day Action Plan:

1)

2)

3)

4)

5)

BONUS for YOU!

Ignite Success: Embrace Agile Change Leadership with the V.I.C.T.O.R. Framework.

Is your team facing challenges that hinder your progress? Do you find it challenging to optimize your idea-to-market cycle? Imagine equipping your leaders with the principles of agile change leadership, empowering them to transform your product management and workflow processes. Look no further – I offer you a game-changing solution: Agile Change Leadership with the V.I.C.T.O.R. Framework, a proprietary methodology designed to unlock your team's potential, accelerate your time to market, and streamline implementation.

As a leader, it's crucial to adapt to the dynamic business landscape. That's why I specialize in teaching leaders like you the principles of agile change leadership. With the V.I.C.T.O.R. Framework, you'll learn how to successfully navigate from idea to market, leveraging resistance as a catalyst for growth and unlocking your team's untapped potential.

Our innovative approach focuses on increasing the quality and speed of your product launches while ensuring implementation is seamless and thorough. By embracing the principles of agile change leadership through the V.I.C.T.O.R. Framework, you'll witness remarkable improvements in efficiency and productivity.

V.I.C.T.O.R. stands for Vision, Innovation, Collaboration, Transformation, Ownership, and Resilience – the core pillars of our methodology. Through this framework, I guide leaders in creating a vision that inspires, fostering a culture of innovation, and promoting collaboration among teams. We transform your organization, ensuring everyone takes ownership of their roles and tasks while building resilience to navigate challenges.

Imagine a future where your team thrives on change, embraces innovation, and delivers exceptional results. The V.I.C.T.O.R. Framework will equip your leaders with the knowledge and tools to drive transformative outcomes. By implementing agile change leadership principles into your product management and workflow management, you'll witness heightened collaboration, improved communication, and accelerated time-to-market.

The benefits of adopting the V.I.C.T.O.R. Framework are manifold. You'll experience reduced time-to-market, improved customer satisfaction, and increased team engagement. By cultivating a culture of continuous improvement and learning, you'll position your organization for long-term success in the rapidly evolving market.

Don't let your team struggle or your ideas fall short. Empower your leaders with Agile Change Leadership using the V.I.C.T.O.R. Framework. Contact me today to schedule a consultation, and together, we'll embark on a journey to unlock your team's true potential, revolutionize your idea-to-market cycle, and achieve unparalleled success. Let's embrace change and forge a path toward a thriving future for your organization.

Let's PowerChat on a FREE Consultation Call! (https://calendly.com/visiontoreality/powerchat-with-yvette-c-owens)

About the Author: Yvette C Owens

EXECUTIVE BIOGRAPHY
Yvette C Owens is a world-renowned speaker, international best-selling author, and leadership coach/consultant who teaches leaders the principles of change leadership to increase adoption, retain talent, and build high-performing teams using the proprietary V.I.C.T.O.R. framework.

The "Business Ambassador"
DestinySpeak Inc.
Helping Leaders Create Healthy Cultures Through Strategic Change

BOOKING CONTACT
Phone: +1 860 778 8524
Email: destinyspeakv2r@gmail.com
Website: destinyspeak.com
Location: Windsor, CT

SOCIAL MEDIA
Facebook: @DestinySpeakV2R
Twitter: @YvetteOwens1
Instagram: @destinyspeak
Store: @DestinySpeakInc
LinkedIn: @yvetteowensbusinessambassador

CORPORATE & BUSINESS
Yvette C Owens is a world-renowned speaker, international best-selling author, leadership coach, and consultant who

teaches change leadership principles to increase adoption, retain talent, and build high-performing teams using the proprietary V.I.C.T.O.R. framework Yvette, AKA Changologist, is a board-certified change management professional (A.C.M.P.). She has 40+ years of sharing her vibrant, resilience, compassion, and influence in teaching how to "Dealing With Resistance To Accept And Invest In Change" during keynote speeches and live and virtual working sessions.

PROFESSIONAL AFFILIATIONS
- CCMP Certified Change Management Professional
- SAFe Scaled Agile
- Certificate of Brand Ambassador-Lifetime Excellence
- Award International
- National Mentoring Program
- Connecticut Partnership Mentoring Program

MEDIA
- CNTV
- Centerpost Media Daily Show
- Hoinser Magazine World Book of Peace 2022
- International Women's Magazine, Hoinser Media
- Meticulous Moments Podcast
- Authors Millionaire Academy Broadcast
- The Douglas Coleman Show VE
- Hoinser Book Queens 2021
- And more…

SPEAKER HIGHLIGHTS
- Catalent Pharma Solutions
- SCORE Western Massachusetts
- CREC Schools
- Kingdom Business Academy
- Women Soar Summit
- Hartford Women's Leadership Summit
- The Kapptor Connection Conference
- Les Brown Online Sales Summit
- TAG Talks VIP Speaker
- Connected Leaders Academy
- And more…

CLIENTS

"You were totally awesome, Yvette Owens. Thank you for joining us and sharing your knowledge and insight." ~ Karen Lincoln, Catalent Pharma Solutions

---

"Yvette is an extremely competent professional with a track record of execution excellence. She is focused on enabling others to deliver as promised in a project leadership context and values getting to the root cause vs. being distracted by symptoms that can drain resources and add risks to scheduling. She is a dynamic speaker and creates a level of confidence amongst leadership that she is driving the effort toward success.

She is known to be a big-picture professional and wants to understand how she can deepen her tool set toward current or future assignments. The most recent example I am aware of is her desire to pursue the CCMP program/designation. She set a goal and maneuvered the organization such that she made it happen.

When I think of Yvette, the characteristics that immediately come to mind are Talented, Depth, Communicator, Smart, Capable and Thought Leader." ~Kevin Nicholson, Lean-N2-InsurTech

---

"Yvette is very knowledgeable in project management and professional development. On several occasions, Yvette customizes training for my team. She took the necessary time to understand my objectives and the needs of my team and over delivered. Yvette is at the top of my list for professional development consulting and project management. I highly recommend Yvette." ~ David Daye, Goodwin University

---

"Yvette takes great pride in her work. She cares about not only achieving the results but getting the desired result the right way with integrity, collaboration, and hard work." ~Mike McNally, Foremost A Farmers Insurance Company

---

"Yvette is a very detail-oriented project manager with exceptional skill at managing multiple deliverables at the same time. In addition to being a highly skilled project manager and staff manager, she is absolutely wonderful to work with. I would highly recommend Yvette for any project." ~ Matt Sweeney, ACE Group

---

"My memorable moment was, you are in control of your destiny. My takeaways are you are valuable, identify your gift and goals, and pursue your purpose." ~ Gwen Neal, Seat of Power Event Attendee

---

"Absolutely amazing…thank you so much! So important for morale." ~ LaVerne Littles, Company Culture with Yvette C Owens Podcast Listener

BOOK REVIEWS OF CONQUERING CORPORATE ENEMIES: MIND. PERSONALITIES. SITUATIONS.

"I read your book. It moved me. Thank you for putting yourself out there. I experienced several very similar scenarios that you described. Other scenarios you talked about I have not and have no words for. It's gross and such a shame, and I'm sorry it all happened to you. I am so inspired by you and how you have dealt with it all and in the ways that you are choosing to move forward. I want to support you and your endeavors tangibly." ~ Carolyn Theriault

"I saw your book on LinkedIn and downloaded it on Kindle. I read the entire thing in one day! Thank you for having the courage to write it and share your experiences and stories." ~ Erica Dougall

"You Nailed It! Addressing the issues of workplace discontent and challenges is not an easy topic. However, the author has done a great job of addressing these complicated situations." ~ Lady Diva T

"I wanted to thank you for paving the way for other African-Americans/West Indians. Your strength, intelligence, and perseverance have made you a great role model. I know I would not survive walking in your shoes. Thank you, and continue being who you are because you are an inspiration. ~ Lisa Mair

www.ingramcontent.com/pod-product-compliance
Lightning Source LLC
Chambersburg PA
CBHW071213120626
46546CB00006B/2543